SAILOR

James Benton

Winter Goose
PUBLISHING
where words take flight

"In *Sailor*, James Benton follows the siren song of imagination across the dark, broad seas of memory and into the unknown. Those who join him on this voyage will be asked to 'learn a fresh new language'—part seaman's jargon, part wave-roar and surf-hiss, part silence. Benton's ear is extraordinary, and like a true sailor he constantly takes soundings of his medium, measuring language to the level of the syllable. From dusty ports of call to colorful bazaars to amorous liaisons in dark rooms, these powerful poems navigate the full range of human emotion in a rhythm that carries the reader along in its current."

—Joshua McKinney, author of *Mad Cursive*

"All hands on deck for Jim Benton's stunning and evocative *Sailor*! Intellectually and imagistically adventurous, Benton's poems beautifully sound the depths of our relationships—both with the human and natural worlds."

—Peter Grandbois, author of *Domestic Disturbances*

"James Benton's *Sailor* is as rollicking a book as a three-day sail through an Indian Ocean cyclone. In poem after poem, the assailed human ship finds itself seized by forces as immense and terrifying as the ocean itself, and as often beautiful and enchanting as the aftermath of a great storm."

—David Axelrod, author of *What Next, Old Knife?*

Winter Goose Publishing
45 Lafayette Road #114
North Hampton, NH 03862

www.wintergoosepublishing.com
Contact Information: info@wintergoosepublishing.com

Sailor

First Edition, January 2017

Cover Design by Winter Goose Publishing
Typesetting by Odyssey Books

ISBN: 978-1-941058-58-9

Published in the United States of America

CONTENTS

HOME

"And how is a sea made?"
—Pablo Neruda

Photo # NH 97953-KN "Old Salt of the Sixth Fleet". Artwork by Frank E. Zuccarelli, 1972

Geese to Fish

Dozens bend their necks
in unison, beat their awkward
lake-bound wings toward the sea,
feet like scaly landing gear
tuck in the slipstream
safety of a migratory formation.

Up-currents buoy them.
Feathers fall away to ash.

Dozens twitch their stunted wings
in unison, arch their unformed
feet toward the shore,
skin like feathered leather
glinting in the jet stream
bonds of a secret formation.

Up-currents buoy them.
Scales fall away to ash.

Hundreds balance on the scale
of air and water—
an awkward bond of migratory secrets—
safety like a leather mouth
barking in formation.

Up-currents buoy them.
Men rise from the ash.

On Thirty-Ninth Street

In the spring, I drive a plastic car up and down my parents' knees while they lay in bed. It's dark. This wakes them and we drive up and down the covers until breakfast. We eat plums from the backyard tree, thick purple flesh. The woman next door never comes outside; she yells if we play too close, too loud. Her window screens smell like dust under a parent's bed.

Across the street, Pearl wears black dresses with white lace at the neck; Thin Frenchie smells of something sour like milk gone tired in the open air too long. You know them. Their porcelain terriers guard the porch. Glass giraffes graze at bowls of hard candy no one eats. Plastic cars line the mantle. They give me one, and they talk with my mother about plums and dust.

***

A boy swings his arms, same time, front to back as he walks down the street, arms like sympathetic neighbors scraping their metal rakes, piling fall leaves in great, rotting mounds for the city to haul away. I ask my mother what's wrong with him. Nothing, she says. He just likes to do it that way. And that settles it.

When I climb behind the wheel of my father's big car, set it rolling down the drive, into Pearl and Frenchie's yard, the woman next door uses one arm to open the door, the other to pull me out. She yells. Her hard fingers smell of plums.

Wrench Bushes

He started early in the day that summer, and, like always, never asked our help. Cats hid under the shrubs to escape the heat, lounged in the acacia branches overhead, scouting our pigeons in the coop. The cats kept watch on Dad in his t-shirt, grime, and the red dome of his baked head. He pulsed to the rhythm the sides of the hot swamp cooler made against his tools.

His tools: he complained a lot about the screwdriver trees growing in the yard back at our last house, popping up from where me and my brother buried the screwdriver seeds. Next to the wrench bushes, probably. To this day, we're mystified by tools, the two of us.

So there he was, forehead like a fire engine, one crescent hammer, wrestled that steel box, huffed it into place, hooked up the water line, and plugged it in to keep his family cool when it was hot enough to roast a cat. Oh, he cussed like a scalded swab-jockey, kicked the steel box, stomped frothing to the kitchen for the bleach to cure the soggy remains of that missing feline stuck all winter in the blower drum. We called him Atticus for that—as if that day he could rise up whole and part the sky. We left his tools alone too, once he cooled off, goddammit.

Folsom Lake, 1975

We remember us upside down, above the lake,
surrounded by strands of grass, damp, matted
flat beneath my back and your knees. Moonlight
spills upon your back and my knees,
your hair and
your eyes and
your upturned chin toward the pewter light.
Our knees swathed in damp grass.

Cool light leaps off your back, your hands sweep across the lake,
a dish of molten silver splashes at its rim.
Oaks erupt with praise and wave to the matted grass swathed
in strands of silver.
Hair spills in the blue night, shadowless.
Your upturned mouth a half-uttered halting
at the rim of a dish of silver lapping at your back,
my back toward the quiet oaks, their hushed limbs spent.

The grass matted in repose, the molten silver
            upturned
shadowless, like your damp hair in the cool light
sweeping low across the freshly matted grass
beneath the oaks hunching at the rim of the lake.

Water laps where the grass gives way to the moon,
staring back at itself as though it had eyes—like ours—to
proclaim itself.

A Nuclear Family

It should have come as no surprise, but while
The children in the front room knelt beside
Their father in his leather chair and prayed,
Their tiny voices whispered up their fears
To his rheumy glares and sour whiskey breath,
His knuckle bones and broken fingernails,
His day-long whiskers rasping at their cheeks—
This family hour, this Norman Rockwell moment
Meant to salvage Daddy from his week-
Long rage of endless venal sins and bathe
His guilt in radiance. It should have come
As no surprise when one reluctant penitent
Slipped out unnoticed from his father's side
And crept in silence to a safer room
Where knuckle bones might never reach, and light
Compressed until it turned to blackened stone.
And there he contemplated his own hands,
Their future worth, their shape and strength, and ran
His fingers through the dark. So then it came
As no surprise when, having chosen not
To tolerate another night of pain
And hopeless prayer, he chose to strike a match
And creep back to his pious kin to wait.

Two Houses

Within sight of the interstate, Rye Valley,
a house lies down: white shiplap, peeled
paint nine layers deep, nothing plumb,
canted over under its own weight.
The homestead is closed, its keeper a late
arriver and true believer in the code of men.

While the place stood, the old man lived
at the top of narrow stairs, light spiked through loose hard-
ware from beneath the plank door.
The window above the fire escape overlooked
a bench swing, still as the dust-hung air,
            overlooked
the terraced cattle tracks surrounding it all
cut in from creek-bed to crest.

There, the old man left a braided whip
coiled like shed skin, a box of shotgun shells
            fading.
Rows of dog-eared daydreams roast by the wedge
            of sun
knifing through the window, the print
of their crackled leaves baked in. His hands rubbed to saddle
leather and rope burns,
rope like stalks of sage.
Salt, bacon, wheat cakes, cattle . . .
Pungency and pain too baked in
to register in this vast, absorbent turf.

The wind is now the memory of brothers
and cousins, and in-laws, and laughter in August looping off
the porch, sticking
in the low hanging willow.

In the beginning—
a half-day's walk up the draw—
read by kerosene, sleep by starlight, dream by
          horsehide,
a shimmer in the ear when knife meets bone, snake hostel,
shotgun zone—its terraced hillside
looks down on the old man rising now and then as a braided
coil of sand.

From the interstate, in summer, some might
          happen
to see great hands reaching
from the rocks where two houses fell,
more apparition than ancestor, proud, defeated:
bent heat
          leather gloves
                    burnt Stetson

Give Me a Flag

1.

I declare myself guilty of never having
to take action, to live in transparency.
Aimless, I roam among revisions
seeking someone who touches stone
and does not return power

to the sea. Unknown by
hands that work only with tools, hard
here in the tree it sings:
the hand is the word
making use of my body.

I was going to crumple up this word
in this ship when I was very young.
I went astray in the world
when victory came too late. My brothers do not know how I
witnessed the quietude of poverty.

I burned nothing but a bitter sheet of paper
at the edges of exactitude, asking
who started this war
that repeats itself once every humid springtime?
It is ink that occupies me,
not to strike a blow of fire,
to pound in the morning.

The day is flat, made smooth
by your apathy. Give me a flag's
mute strength, the trees tell me.
I tell my hands so many things
about how a sea is made,
how I worked hard to keep
still, knowing one hand makes a mutiny.

SINGAPORE

"Ignorance is the parent of fear."
—Ishmael

Sailor

1.

Herded from airport to bus, the riot windows
wired shut; from bus to bunkhouse,
rows of empty bunks wall-to-wall.
Herded in single file past a steel-mesh window,
told to write our last address
on a label they tape on a box.
I have only one bag, which they put
in a box and ship home.

Herded to the third floor and seated in rows,
whispering together in low light,
we shift, elbow to shoulder, for an inch
more space and hunker into ourselves.
our eyes dart through the dark
for a sign, and we sniff at the air:
the smell of apricots rises from the floor.

2.

He stomps into the room, one foot dragging,
to the podium where he waits, wordlessly, for
            quiet.

Who is this man with his beard like Ahab,
cocking his white hat to the back of his head?

With his weight on his good leg, he unloads his
stories,
his thick hand stabs the podium until it cracks.

He is the gnome of Thailand, the Popeye of
Guam,
Narcissus of Midway and the South China Sea,

sent to redeem us from squalls west of Singapore
and lead us not into port calls of women and
drink.

As though he already knows us by name,
kindred and willing, tamed and lulled,

he talks of honor, and duty, and grief, until two
in the morning when our eyes quit darting and
adjust to the dark.

A dangerous smell like apricot fades from the
room,
and we dock a few merciful seconds of sleep at
the end of day one.

3.

We learn a fresh new language.
A floor is a deck, while hatches are holes
in a deck, not a wall, which turns out is a
bulkhead, and the head is where
a company goes to shower and shave.
Heel-to-toe is now "nut-to-butt"

so the line to the galley is quiet and quick.
Our black shoes are sky blue unless there are
clouds,
and then they are white.
Gasping and sore, we are "running-through
Georgia"
not in boots, but in boondockers, in covers, not
hats
we drill on the grinder with pieces, not rifles.
Our clothing is gear we stow "up-to and
touching."
Everything stenciled and newly named
in case we forget—names like
Drowdy, Dennison, Sieving, Penn,
Gunderson, Miller, Bullington, Groot.

Fire

All elbows on deck,   klaxon
loose bootlaces
caps askew,   what time?
drop
everything not a tool   now
drop
everything burnable
drop   everything   klaxon
not a drill

Below the glowing fo'c'sle
Black smoke   rolls at us—   overhead
Black smoke   through the passageway
A stinking steel-   wool blanket,   the thing rolls
black pillow   case, mouth
agape

ember tongue—
we lope together into it, purified
Signalman engineman
boatswain and all of us steady
Elbows and reflex and nothing
that isn't a tool.

We crouch at the hot hatch like a shield
T-shirts, gloves, leather coats, masks,
Hoses drool readiness
We take instructions: elbows tucked
Cool that hatch,
Un-dog it hinge-side before
It blisters shut.

eyes like
And the hatch jumps open thimbles of sand

We throw fans, and lightning, and rope
We throw our teeth in desperation wide

We throw foam at it like prayer

We choke it off at its throat

wailing

For hours.   Brother,   we

wear its char in our lungs like a map of grace.

gnashing

klaxon

Plain Trade

It's late and you should go.
But before I get my wallet,
I ask again, who would choose this life,
sold to the point a cold vacuum
consumes all pulsing heat,
until, having convulsed its last,
nothing remains even to burnish.

One wretched uncle cannot be enough
apprenticeship, not the neighbor
kid down the block with the braces.
Not the heat of a first innocent
kiss, not like an uncle, heat
that ends in torn shirts and wrenched fingers,
not the thousand kisses after and
after layers deep. That shame
withers against a cheek no one believes you
broke reaching for the soap. I barely notice
the bruise in this light that likewise hides my own.

Won't you say, for a fee,
what vast weight crushed
that last gram, that hint, of grace?
In this quiet vacuum we are not gifts
to give without rage but ragged commodities.
For my fee we might reclaim without remorse
a faint flicker of dignity
that snuffed itself long ago in an unseen,
unloved, winking out.

In this wordless transaction,
your voice is thick paper slishing in your palm,
a purse snapping shut, a door.

I see that you have reached
the temperature of bondage reduced to embers
—fair exchange.

Ivory and Opium

The dragon has abandoned this place,
the stone gate fallen from the wall.
Unguarded, the shrines smoke
empty and wooden as my grandfather's first
memory of the old ones when
the dragon watched
and kept the stone strong.

In this archway here, their bony
spindles, by oil glow, tossed
the tiles. Their incense drew
me as a boy from
the shadowed corner to watch.
Hot stems hung steaming from their contented
grins.

In this way, I was to pass the ivory and opium
down to my son.
I would show you the old coins,
or the broken tortoise shells.
The bronze is dead, the yellow ivory brittle as it
falls.
The dragon unhinged this place long ago.

Dolphin Song

A splitting apart warns the water
and the fish that beg to speak
of the rumbling earth below—
a deep saline connection breaking.

Kelp throws its dead ashore
in desperation. Coral skeletons cling
welded to volcanic rock. Brainless
organisms know hot ash-damp
hardening into mountain roads.

Crying dolphins wake the morning village.
Long, blue, plasma-streaked sand
bands of darkness flee the slick flesh
and low sun. Old men
drop their nets; their weak tendons
strung on bone pop hemp-like against
the tide of squealing fish.
We read the rotting scrawls
of blue meat. Vagrant
elders watch from the sea wall.
They nod. They rise.
They scuttle across the sand
in their wisdom to join the exodus.

Cannibals

What would I have my daughter take from you
my vanquished, my hero—
a piece of flesh, a bone?
You were powerful when the spirit quickened you.
Your eyes owned the secret beauty
of places she may one day conquer;
your shoulders bent to the work of attaining them.
Your heart possessed the will and anguish of
enduring.

And I will have my daughter

consume it all. In your
name she will partake of your
body she will assume your
place in time and spirit.

For I will name you to her
and she will devour your eyes and your shoulders.

I will name her for you
and she will carry your anguish in her heart.
I will name her for you.

COLOMBO

"That one striveth, this one jetteth all in vain."
—Ishmael

Indian Ocean: Day Three

A bass breaks free of gravity ahead of the storm.
Sailors scramble fore to aft, bracing for
a wash of green foam loaded with debris. A rage
    of rain.
Beyond the cold fusion of hydrogen, oxygen,
and salt, a profusion of fish and phosphor
slaps against the steel. Primordial soup clings to
    the painted
skin in grit layers like finely lacquered emery paper
glinting in the hard rain. The whole edifice tips
on an axis adrift, a compass misaligned,
a plate askew, a chair on end, a door
flailing too near a sleeping outstretched
arm. Some riders harness themselves to a rack;
    others
shim themselves into wedges
hard against the heaving sea. Some read lurid
books, write letters home to Mother. Hands like
    knots pulled thin
and white, thin and white around a rope. Engines
groan against their own reluctance. The ship
    lurches upward, hangs
for an ictus of time, then plunges forward while
a sea bass breaks across the bow.

Shore Power

Our detail is a tug-of-war with three twisted
copper braids, sheathed in rubber and rope,
spooled in salt-crusted, hundred-foot lengths:
a three-spined electric core uncoiling into our hands.

Its oiled hide slips across our thighs,
its belly binds against a stanchion.
Black and crackling, bucking and hissing,
it buckles in waves at the threshold of a door.

Twelve men, rancid with ache,
heave to, glove over glove,
bones bending, fever bursting from our backs.
We crawl in place to haul it ashore,
bridle it with rope, unbraid its convulsions,
cradle it, drag it straight, make it yield.

We string it, sixteen pounds to the foot, head to
tail.
It hangs between hawsers barking against their
cleats,
and once subdued, fang to socket,
we cowl it with canvas against weather and rats,

and then—gently, as though it might strike—then
we ignite it.

Picasso Was an X-Man

That first stroke made them look. How it began
low and to the left, from an athletic squat,
and then rose like the trajectory of artillery fire
as he stood, recalling news of Guernica,
how he swooped the arm, turned the hip,
balanced the weight of the line on the ball of his
    foot,
shifting like crosswind and rage,
until there it was:
a perfect arc, in perfect proportion to his pain.
Blind, drunk, and effortless.

Runners at the Ready

The runners crouch alone in staggered lanes
in breathless solitude and wait. A wash
of sound begins to swell and mask their pounding
heartbeats, and familiar voices fade
into translucence. Then they measure out
the distance from desire to desire,
from poise and early promise, to the sprint
around the lined and level track
where all is silence but the fog of breath,
the practiced, fluid motion of the hands,
the memory of the countless measured steps
of all the runners who have come before.
How quickly athletes close the gap
between them, one in front and one in back.
And now the one begins to slow, and now
the other matches pace until they touch
across a shrinking continent.
                                        And this
is how a great and heavy thing is passed.

Olive Tree

per il mio antenato da Lucca, Abdanego

It came down to the trees' twisted hands
that pulled their sinews up
from the land's thin crust. Hands
that cut timbers shaped with gouge
and mallet, stained with oil
and sage, heavy-scented, torn slabs
thick with scar, straightened with eye and rasp.

He worked alone, this happy genuflection.
Steel and branch yielded to some
crossed mimic of his want,
to his hint of da Vinci straining
to the music of spheres,
toward a wonderment of generations
pressing through the gnarl of his olive
hands at work. He asked what lodestone brought
him to this soil to show the sun
his teeth yellow from olive pressing, his eyes
raised like ascension,

legs bowed by the strain of timbers
hauled and mitered to a pure
precision, thankful for toil, grateful
for endurance, eager for release. His legacy
a stout cross standing before pews jointed square
as the hands that built them—
his vanishing in the seams of my father's face.

MIDWAY

"The greater idiot ever scolds the lesser."
—Ahab

Midway Women's Bowling League

We didn't call him "Stinky" yet; that came after
shore patrol shut the drunken picnic down
and he chose to dash naked across
eight lanes of hardwood, dodging
sniper fire bowling balls, women shooting
at this pink and fuzzy arcade target scampering
out the back door where Sanders was
supposed to be with the clothes but wasn't
and the next move hadn't quite been planned,
so he improvised, flapping
bare feet on concrete slapping,
before the women howling,
before the sirens closing in,
before—thinking naked was a joke
and failing to plan ahead—
he jumped the levee into the muck,
and how they returned him to us:
wearing only his new hero's name.

Bull Riding at Sea

I tell a story of riding waves
at the bow of a ship in a bitch of a storm.
Not in the way a surfer wants,
with grace and skill, lifted by tides
balanced between airborne and grounded,
steering her board by shifting her weight,
a *pas de deux* in aquamarine.

No, this is more
the way a cowboy rides a cinched bull
loose and huge and angry, and me
clenched to the wire rail, hoping
my leather gloves take the deep cut,
heels braced against the leaping gunwale
while the swells groan and bank and throb—
a living and indifferent thing.

I tell of plunging with a twisted shudder
into a wall of sharp horizon lashing out,
gale-whipped and dark as madness.
I tell of conceding to the bull
after a single round, once was rare enough, I say.
Certain claims seem fair to make.
I've told of this stunt so often it might even be true.

Going Fifty-Five

Another day, another seven cents,
Another weary turn around the wheel,
Another paisley tie to help you feel
As though you might one day relent
And join the workforce here. But no, you spent
Down to your food allowance on that seal-
Skin Maserati, and the girls in heels
Until some kink inside forced you to repent.

We wish you'd stuck around a little longer—
You were fun at parties. But we heard
You'd gotten canned and shaved your head
Or some such thing and that you grew a beard,
Tattooed your neighbor's thigh before you fled.
Tell me how it felt, and make me stronger.

The Haight

We haven't yet been gentrified
          this street and I:
our tired slogans sprayed on
          plywood windows
a batik shop, out of place
          shot with sandalwood
haunted by cats. Patchouli
          hangs like bait
above the fractured bay.
          Say what you will, children,
nothing is free. Not shelter
          from fog, nor shoes,
nor lungs wracked with hacking.

Self Portrait

This is the one whose portrait
includes a bullwhip,
the one who built an eyeless plastic
          friend with latex tongue,
the one with blindfolds, high heels, fishnet,
lying on her back and breathing bathtub
          water for our amusement.

At first, we thought she was courageous to appear
like that, naked,
to die with every breath
before the camera's surrogate eye,
courage that kept her trying,
kept her trying to almost drown,
to gasp, to choke, to sputter and rise,
to peek out from the video loop
and release for us, repeatedly, that faint
private
smirk.

The Company You Keep

Whatever dead men say is always true,
Their voices, soft and silver. In your ear,
However lifelike they may sound to you,

They're but a mirror of the things you do;
They return to urge and stoke your fear.
Whatever's dead, men say, is always true

For accusations hurled at them. You knew
What set us both apart, yet kept us near,
However rational it sounds to you,

Was only partial sanity. You threw
Away the part of me you held most dear.
Whatever. Dead men say it's always true

That what is right is never absolute,
That lies you tell become the lies you hear,
However righteous they may sound to you.

Now as I hear you speak, I'll have a few
Regrets to hurl backward. I'll endure
Whatever dead men say—it's always true,
However lifelike I may sound to you.

DJIBOUTI, KARACHI

"I am tormented with an everlasting
itch for things remote."
—Ishmael

Photo # NH 47029-A (without poem) "Spinning a Yarn" on board USS Enterprise, circa 1887

Sharing a *Gitanes* with a Stranded Turkish Sailor Waiting for His Ship to Return

I find myself in the French Territory of Afars and Issas, this place of little value except for an accident of geography. Wedged between Somalia and Ethiopia, it is simultaneously both and neither, but it occupies an extraordinarily important strategic spot at the entrance to the Red Sea in the Gulf of Aden. The stone facades of the colonial marketplace lie vacant, abandoned by the French, and ignored by the Africans. Rows of crumbling masonry stand as the public face of empty tombs, shuttered, sealed, the streaked window glass baked to opacity.

Is liquor sufficient souvenir? More action than trinket, more verb than noun?

Nothing grows here. There is no shade, no pollen in the air; inertia alone holds the sullen earth in place. Everything is dust, or about to become dust, or it is covered over or filled with dust. The torpid wandering of the destitute kicks loose hot wisps of the stuff, which clogs the nostrils and coats the skin until there is only the smell of dust, and skin fades to the neutral color of the vast landscape itself. In this chromatically desaturated condition, race disappears altogether, and our differences emerge only when the loudspeaker on the minaret sparks to life. Even then, we are the same in our humble solemnity, each of us bowing in awe at the overwhelming insignificance of our petty desires.

At the base of a long, sloping avenue lies a broad district of decrepitude, wriggling with activity.

African Street

Five times daily, he will face Mecca
sallow-cheeked and sunken-eyed,
kiss the parched gray dirt to pray,
a mantis on his shoulder
praying too.

He stands. He knee-crack walks
beyond the brickwork street,
a gas lamp streaks the husking
night home.

With his goats and children
one more empty sack of flour
will make a door to keep
out the eyes to his tin shack.

Ten o'clock, and children clump
in doorways, chasing strangers
counting toothless English
in pursuit.
Mantis vein-lined leafy wings
bend and turn in the swirling
gray-blue sky.
Its reverent, hungry claws
grab at snap-skinned flies:
drops of drying pain.

Had they prayed too, perhaps
their vengeful God would
never have come.

Karachi

All the dust between your limbless birth
and the marketplace has settled in your weave,
a bundle of rags left
on the street   near a door   you
bowl of coins: you
loose-wrapped wad, you
cotton shard. You
kicked from the road, the sweat
on a donkey's hide, you
burnt bed of woven rope lit by
amber ropes of light.
The dye bakes from bright red to gray,
to burnt gray from yellow brocade.
The husk of the sun rouses even this
living bag of laundry someone
carries daily to the street when
morning is coolest and foot traffic highest
past the chipped bowl. I
leave you to your verbless life,
those flint eyes blinking
from behind their mask of rags, you torso—
collecting the day alone beside a bowl of coins.

As You Leave Me

Fallen and cracked
you clutch your hands to your ears,
your eyes go dull as a sheet
drawn up beneath the lids,
your hand flutters as your spirit pulls away.
You've spilled your coffee—
Do you hear me?

The horizon has faded to smoke,
there are voices, I think:
yours, mine, maybe others.
My knees are damp from the ground.
Some rain—
Do you know? Is there something you know?

I think for an instant to rest
my hand, a gesture of mercy
in your wrinkled silence,
to your mouth, your nose—
Is it time?
I smooth away the rain from your eyes,
warm your ears, dry your hair.
Perhaps you can hear through the gauze of ice
some quiet voice near your face
murmuring to you as memory.
Is it time? Is it time?

Cornucopia

The horn of plenty is a granite heap streaked
with gold. Miners dug it out of holes, milled it to
dust—
to dust from pounded dust. Hammer and fire,
anvil and tong, slag in the weave of their sleeves
measured in grams per ton.
Mining pulls the insides out,
tearing a hole where veins once had lain.

Mining is a hard thing.

Now the mountain clutches
its gold, and the bear grass blankets
a sinew of rusted cable, a twisted post, a concrete
slab.

Your mother loved the fragile silence of this place,
broken by the slap of water in a cobbled creek,
the transport of lovers echoing off the mountain
face,
the ring of iron tongs bolting through the fir trees.

You went there to measure how
a mountain stands erect, how
she yields her treasure at the cost
of scarred knuckles and cut bone.

You went there to return her,
inched along the fallen
log above the stream strewn with rock.

You went there, a thimbleful of ash
in a hard stone streaked with gold.

And then you broke
open the stone, pulled the insides out,
gave back an arc of sand,
cut bone stamp-milled to dust.

Mining leaves a hole and a pile of scree.
In the shadow of a mountain, you did a hard
thing.

Iris Petals

Your home when last I saw you was a splendid
Specimen of order: a delicate sketch of an iris
Wrapped in ivy, driftwood in an ebony frame,
A Nautilus under glass, a china bowl—

To see you now, shirtless, lashed to your bed,
machines
Sticking from hip to chin, plastic tubes, electric
Probes ticking, whirring—the purple seam
You wear on your chest like penance—
Whose demon have they carved from your ribs?

In your dreams, in your confessions of pain
Did your father wear a shroud like yours?

You said you wanted to lure him with wine,
Lead him to the basement, bind him with rope,
Have him wake to the dark, to eyes purple with
rage.
You dreamed of chains, and granite walls fitted
with steel,
You, the railing surgeon unmoored and mad.
What sins of his did you hope to purge
With your vengeance of flails and knives?

A single iris blooms on the nightstand near
The monitor, garish under the florescent glare.
Petals wrap like loose skin around its hollow stem
And bend toward the dim light, and you
With iodine stains and a wrist band to know you
by.

The Bridge

It's vertigo   that bridge   orange
gravity and seduction,
yes, and so
orange

the heavy arc of wire under post
and pillar, arc over blue water
cold and deep below that flaking
bridge. Fog over the hard towers
under the crow sky, fog behind
the eyes, their lids fast as traffic

red

as   foggy sweaters   dim
as the bob and jog
of wool caps passing
gray like pavement
headlights
like an iris   wide and staring
over the rail   arc of gulls
cool on the wings   wide
into the   vertigo   wide
as arms slipping past
altogether.

Cousins

". . . with all thine offerings thou shalt offer salt."
—Leviticus, 2:13

Tell me if it was the rock salt or the tannins
leeched
from the old oak barrel that dried your heart.
Beside the shed, four years old, laughing,
we ate handfuls of it drawn by an urgent sting
to suck the rain off the clean edges.
I was amazed by your disjointed thumbs, your
teeth
lightning white and horse-grin wide,
you begged from hunger on the car trip
back from fishing; fed hay to horses
in your backyard; leaped hooting into the pool.
In the dark, you lit a flashlight in your mouth:
tooth-shadow, vein-pulse, pumpkin-shell—
This is how I know you.

Perhaps in time the orange rust that stained the
salt
stained your tongue and like a dry poultice pulled
away your resolve: pure rock shot through with
seams.

Were you thirsty, salt-washed, rock-salt cooled,
rock hard?
Did it grind away your teeth melting in your
cheeks?
Did it sharpen your blood, nick your veins from
inside?

Did it streak your dry-bone hide with years of raw
salt, and scrub your dreams to a crust of flecks?

Tell me what alchemy of rust and rain and oak
drew you, the way a poultice draws a nettle's
          urgent sting,
to a hidden copse of aspen shuddering
between the rain above and the salt below, where
          you cooled
the iron barrel against your raw salt tears,
and stained the ground orange, shot through.

HOME

"... his homecoming is at hand,
when he shall see his dearest,
and walk on his own land."
—Homer

Give Me a Flag

2.

I declare myself guilty
of never having this ship
strike a blow of fire
to witness the quietude of poverty.
This sea is flat, made smooth.

From your remnants, give me a flag
of hands that only work machines never
asking how is a sea made,
or who makes use of my body
when no one sees me?

It is ink that occupies me
to take action, to live against the transparency
that when I was very young I went astray
in the world, pounding in the morning,

burning nothing but a bitter sheet of paper.
Strength is mute, the trees tell me, but
here in the swale of a galled ocean it sings,
it reveals itself in humid springtime,
works hard to keep still.
All day someone hammers.

I am going to crumple up this word
roaming aimlessly among revisions
though a victory, it is too late. I do not know,
yet everyone knows the rain,
and still I do not return.

Power of the secret deep
in the edge and in the exactitude
I tell my hands so many things:
the hand is the word—
one hand making mutiny.

Winslow, Arizona

There was this one guy who couldn't wait to get his discharge and go home to Winslow, Arizona. Once, he told me all about how his life there was so much better than what it was here, where all *we* did was look for new places in the Far East to colonize while keeping the Russians from thinking the Indian Ocean was their private bathtub. Nothing serious. But Winslow was better, he told me, and I could tell he meant it by the way he rubbed his head as if it itched real bad. One night, when it was quiet, and the movie had been over for a while, and we had been drinking coffee and generally being pals talking about dumb shit in low voices, he started in on Winslow, Arizona again.

"Yeah, see I was driving my '74 Ranchero, you know, the V-8 model, and I had put a six-barrel carb in it and a racing cam—yeah, that was a great ride. Cherry red. So I was parked over by the Circle K waitin' for Mikey to show up so we could, you know, hang out and stuff, but I guess he was getting into it with his cousin Dan or something, so it musta been around nine thirty or around there. Pretty soon I saw Dan roll through the intersection and pull into the Winchell's across the street, so I fired up the Ranchero and backed out real slow cuz I weren't in no hurry, see, and hung a left coming out of the parking lot and sort of waited at the light for it to turn green. Hell, there weren't any traffic that late, 'specially with the train so slow and blocking the street out by the water tower and all, so I said, 'what the hell,' and just eased her on through anyways, and pulled up next to Dan there in the Winchell's. So we got a couple Winchell's and hung out for a bit, and pretty soon Dan had to get back, so it was just me again. So then, after a little bit I kicked the Ranchero into reverse, and backed on out into the lane, you know, and thought, prob'ly a good time to fill'er up with gas, so I looked over, and the Texaco was still open, and I figured eighty-six cents a gallon wasn't gonna kill me anyways, so I pulled in there and had Slow Eddy fill'er for me. Checked the oil too. That's service the way it oughta be. Not like out here."

He rubbed his head kind of slow, for a minute, thinking real hard. "Yeah, I can't wait to get home," he said with that low voice of his.

The View at Two A.M.

You see him there most days,
my brother,
leaking blood from his eyes
hunched over his work
like a question mark.
The tail of his pen flicks at his face.
The ink near the window
within reach. Ready.
At his easel again,
he scratches frantic marks back
and forth on the page in parallel
like a patch of iron filings seeking north.
"I'm about a hundred hours in to this one," he says.
"I guess it's halfway done."

The edge of the page is a window frame.

You see him there most days
leaking blood from his eyes.
My brother's neighbor:
he's at his window again,
inert, an argon sun, four
black mouths agape, heavy
in silence and brick.
He holds back the curtain,
eyes again the fragile escape
just out of reach.
No one walks the street,
his dark entrance inviolate.
Last week's sleeping cat,
news-pulp leaves,

fetid faucet drippings and unread ink.
In the center of the frame, parked
at the curb, inert, its argon glow reduced to rust,
tail-fins of a gas-drunk monster.

I look at my brother, a question mark
scratching at his easel.
He has misspelled "Cadilac"
in fresh ink, in the center of the frame.

Business as Usual

Let me go down in battle
my heart rattling in its cage
with brown oil caked on a rifle butt.
Let me stand in the grit alone
wince as this one twitches
that one wails and then is silent.

***

Let me go down in battle
not this anteroom where,
at my hand, reams of cold digits
accumulate into a boneyard of
green and white binary columns.
Here, I am dead but not yet counted.

***

Let me go down in battle
not this sanitary corridor
sniveling, thin and senile,
left to roll my tongue in an empty mouth
at the end unable to reach
for a hand to hold.

Domestics

If only it was simple like your shirt
doesn't match your shoes or the newspaper
lies on the table or
even thank you and good
morning grinding up
the beans making coffee simple
as scorching toast. Some of us
beg for mornings like
these, years of this—over
yes and no—years
of dentistry and
surgery and how do you
do and have you heard
our gray hair and none from
what we were and could have been

Proof of Ghosts

hair at first a ring of light
the scrawl of fingers pressed
inside my eyes the scent

of vanilla mixed with your ginger
they are not your eyes
or bones but suspend a pale

predecessor's frame
some dallied youth
recombinant for an hour

throwing dice from a cup
against your firm scroll version

The Art of Lying
Or: "No, they look great on you"

A palimpsest

The opposite of a brick is a hole.
    I want you to be totally honest with me.
Through a broken window, branches
    This won't hurt a bit.
Levitate in clusters.
    I would love it if you did.
Half of a bird
    Of course I remembered.
Calls out while
    I'll give it right back.
Half chases after. Water
    I'm sorry.
Parts in crisp lines or
    Never again.
Falls away sideways.
    Forever.
A pair of eyes dart left of their
    I am your voice in Washington.
Nose above a jagged
    We'll be home by March.
Mouth.
    This is "for the children."

The opposite of a broken window is
    A thorough investigation reveals
true.
    There is no evidence of wrongdoing.

Covenant

Thunder clouds the color of chrome and fire; the
sun
cast over the eastern hills chilled beneath the
overcast.
The air, pale as autumn grass, warps into a beacon
of
scattered violet, and blue, and green, and red.
Shadows of the scrub and waste
sharpen under two arcs of light touching ground
below the tree line, almost in reach.
Painters never quite get them right.

We took it for a covenant,
and almost spoiled it
by speaking.

That morning we were ten again and luminous
with wonder.
Could we stand inside them? Could we touch?
Would they warm our skin, like old dreams,
glancing at the edges of them: soft focus and dust?
We were ten again, and light erupted from open
space.
Light held back the sky.

Heroic Coupling

I see no reason to abate the roving eye
when what you seek refuses to deny
the sidelong glance, the unobtrusive touch.
How fortunate that even after this much
time, the soft sound of corduroy excites
as much as when the promise of delights
to come awakened in us both a blind
desire. The thought of leaving all behind,
of locking arms—and let's admit it, legs—
admitted nothing. Like the tail that wags
the dog, we leashed together yours and mine

and so we prospered for a month or two,
until we woke to find the rent was due,
until the one forgot to dump the trash,
and then the other squandered all the cash,
and bickering ensued, and babies wailed,
and suddenly, when languid lust derailed,
it must have seemed to you we'd lost
the spark that made the effort worth the cost.
Now I admire that roving eye of yours,
the way you look around and reassure
me you remember how it felt
when we were young, and sight alone could melt
the universe like wax, and nothing less.

O Time Thy Pyramids

She dug for earthworms, planted
amaryllis near the barn, cultivated
daylight when the bad boys came to her
and she never sent them home.
For her alone, they spoke in tempered tones
reached for manners as they reached for seed.
She gave them tools to dig with,
voice to their voices, ears to their hearing.
She finished when the work was done,
and then it was time for them to go.
They were safe with this labor of bulbs:
the loam that stuck to her soft gloves
stuck to the bad boys' canvas shoes.
Their shoes took rich earth from her barn,
pieces of the one who never sent them away,
who showed them how to plant crocus,
how to plant even after she'd gone—
their safe tiller in the damp earth—
they became like the best of the boys
she never sent away, the one
            she kept and cultivated until she was gone.

Faded Familiar

We once returned his things
a gift—his badge and belt, his old-style
cap, baton, and leather ticket book preserved
as if museum pieces sealed in amber—
remembrance in a shadow box.
Uniforms hung in a wooden frame.

His job, he said,
            to make his children
competent, our love, if possible
            a bonus in the bargain—

He picked the bloodied broken from the streets
and buried night-shift nightmares in
a cloak pulled tight across his chest.
He built his house, planted the trees,
always drove, sailed boats,
granted marriages—

His eyes have sealed over since,
ears hearing one relentless note,
whose words are not his own,
pulls the grief of history tight across his
faded and familiar countenance.
He aches and knows his wall is falling,
but will not frighten us with an honest account.

The bonus is I tremble at those uniforms inside
that heavy frame.

UNIFIED FIELD THEORY

"... that episode of the imagination
which we call reality."
—Fernando Pessoa

Folding a Mirror

1.

This is not a   poem winter sunsets love.
the moon more than   summer rains hate the.
sun alabaster is the   ring of triumph I.
think wouldn't you but   on any other morning.
that dog would lunge   from behind glass to.
chew at more than   memories drink or wither.
like the alabaster skin   of dogs the old.
crow barked out just   then three more words.
only pay no attention   emerged ragged like this.
meaning nothing special really   not poem but this.

2.

Every other sentence contradicts   the third one back.
horses know it before   Sunday brunch another milksop.
exposes weak penance proven   over coffee spilled on.
the diner floor no   one notices but the.
paper boy do they   have paper boys any.
more than papers anymore   and who would notice.
anyway the wind blows   from the stubbled shore.
of the lake of   fire burns the forest.
before the presses do   no one reads them.

3.

Simple minds ride simple   pleasures and birds there.
is Chicago and here   is San Francisco neither.

is you exactly once   I thought I had.
died and gone to   Mexico or Baja maybe.
in a past past   life sometimes confoundingly there.
is cheese more than   twenty or thirty species.
and subtypes coagulate in   spore cities a site.
of uncontainable peonies attract   ants artichokes attract gnats.
wheat and weevils peat   bogs and meat break.
bread with me.

4.

Some days they pick   up the trash other.
days I don't care   about automobile maintenance shotgun.
repair is another kind   of gardening with fewer.
parts a declarative sentence   is harder to write
than you imagine I   have no idea what.
you imagine do that   math and calculate the.
redundancy of arguing that   we are genetically predis-
posed.
to suffer incompetent mind   readers or would you.
fold a dry mirror   in half for trying.

5.

Who was it asked   about the headlines today.
better than yesterday's do   we call them olds.
as though the conversation   had already engaged the.
distance between two strangers   over coffee empty glasses.
clinkless when rudely jammed   together making bad
chemistry
or target exiles show me   gate to terminal lounge.

6.

Hummingbirds are more angry   than they are meant.
to be light thumbs   of feather and dance.
is a poem in motion   fugues for the eyes.
sprites of endless exercise   machines with blood pumps.
and needle tongues punching   through nectar search
anosmic.
pheromone sources of raw   sugar or die protecting it.

complacency is therefore never   more than six feet.
from catastrophe whose cask   aged drink defiles only.
those who cannot carry   their own weight gold.
induces sleep in those   who have none to.
begin with but shines   like copper after years.
rain that time erodes   even stainless gate keepers.

A Mirror of Hands

I will live to the moon, and there, follow
a musical sky for her. But, returning
to the moon when the sun comes up, I will be
her wavering. She is coming at night
to dead valleys. Hours playing beside a
bridge; beautiful love eating from a clock too
long. Her rooms open to a
waterfront of celestial men—dark
wildflowers she pockets by the castle-full

And when I set fire to her
(Arson in a mirror of hands)
she may yet return
burning into a sparrow's decay
pouring with lost voices
covered in the robes of a youthful brain
singing like lunar blood.

Crow Revisited

1.

The earthquake turned,
tearing the dead into a question mark.
The barred serpent showed
its words turned into bombs:
it had a hare. They slowly took
to the sea bed and
turned to its most hidden part. A good drink
lifting its fruitless key against him,
he leaped for the bunker,
and found his privacy
curled up into the hill.

2.

An earthquake had the key, took it to the bunker,
and showed he could tear apart
a good drink into bombs.
He slowly turned a hare (it tore at
its fish-thing) and found the sea bed
curled up into its most hidden words.
Fruitless, they lifted a dead mole.
It leaped for a question mark—
blasted its privacy:
the hill turned serpent.

Oceanus Pacificus

and see   how our long churn recedes

beyond the eye to the goblet rim
who can doubt its curvature

the wavering chop the interzone
of brine and breath luminescent
below the sun

how broad the chasm of this pinched
perspective we believe our power

enough to preserve us

to deny our nature to fall and
all our effort to remain afloat impaled

upon the grace of an indifferent
sea our boiling tail the trace of our transit
hisses until the last ear

sinks below its unstill yawning
gape hubris rides the slippery spine
world without witness to discover
for once if beyond here dwell dragons

ACKNOWLEDGMENTS

I wish to thank the editors of the following publications, in which several of these poems first appeared, some in earlier versions. Small literary journals are the crucibles in which our culture is annealed.

Oregon East: "Indian Ocean, Day Three," "Covenant," "As You Leave Me," "The View at Two A.M."

Calaveras Station: "Cousins," "Iris Petals," "Folsom Lake, 1975"

Convergence: an online journal of poetry and art: "Shore Power," "Olive Tree," "Karachi," "Domestics," "Proof of Ghosts"

Raintown Review: "Nuclear Family," "The Company You Keep"

Word Riot: "Midway Women's Bowling League"

Poetry Now:"Cannibals," "Self Portrait," "On Thirty-Ninth Street," "Hard Landing"

Flatmancrooked's Slim Volume of Contemporary Poetics: "O Time Thy Pyramids," "Oceanus Pacificus"

Clade Song: "Dolphin Song"

San Pedro River Review: "Wrench Bushes"

Tahoma Review: "Cornucopia"

The Possibility Place: "Two Houses"

PHOTO ACKNOWLEDGMENTS

Old Salt of the Sixth Fleet
Old Salt of the Sixth Fleet Letterpress reproduction of an oil painting by Frank E. Zuccarelli, depicting a Salty Sailor on board USS Strong (DD-758), while on duty with Sixth Fleet in the Mediterranean Sea, July 1972. Courtesy of the Navy Art Collection, Washington, D.C. U.S. Naval History and Heritage Command Photograph.
Catalog #: NH 97953-KN
Public domain image

Singapore
Source: National Archives of Singapore

Colombo
User: Milei.vencel /Wikimedia Commons/CC-by-SA-3.0

Midway
Lt. Comdr. Charles Fenno Jacobs (1904-1975) for the U.S. Navy - General Photographic File of the Department of Navy. National Archives and Records Administration, Local Identifier 80-G-470222 This media is available in the holdings of the National Archives and Records Administration, cataloged under the ARC Identifier (National Archives Identifier) 520883
Public domain image

Djibouti, Karachi
"Spinning a Yarn"
(without verses) Spinning a Yarn Seven Old Salts engaged in telling tall tales aboard USS Enterprise (1877-1909), probably while their ship was at the New York Navy Yard, circa spring 1890. Photographed by E.H. Hart, New York. Suitable verses from The Tale of the Gyascutus are printed below the original photographic image. U.S. Naval History and Heritage Command Photograph.
Catalog #: NH 47029-A
Public domain image

Home
Proof of Ghosts
Photo by the author. © 2002

Unified Field Theory
Source unknown

NOTES

"A Mirror of Hands," "Give Me a Flag," "Creation Myth," and "Crow Revisited" are, in the main, the result of applying the OuLiPo constraint called "Matthew's Algorithm" to various source texts. These sources included Philip Lamantia's "I Am Coming" (for "Arson"), Pablo Neruda's *The Hands of Day* (for "Destiny"), Albert Goldbarth's *Combinations of the Universe* (for "Creation Myth"), and Ted Hughes's *Crow* (for *Crow Revisited).* These source materials I gratefully acknowledge. In addition to subjecting these texts to the OuLiPo machine, the outcomes were further modified by altering some verb forms, changing some nouns altogether, adding new text or deleting resulting language as I saw fit. The objective was to ascertain, if possible, what the new text seemed to want to express, independent of either the original author's intention or my own intention, and then to tease out that meaning through the careful manipulation of the language, syntax, line breaks, and other elements of semantic cohesion in order to produce a wholly new work with a wholly new purpose, message, and voice.

Iris Petals arose from my recent discovery of a strange photograph of an equally strange old friend, gifted artist, dilettante, and part-time libertine, whose history is as exotic as his name.

Covenant: It turns out that the pot of gold lies in the middle of an open field just west of Interstate 84 near North Powder, Oregon. Who knew?

On Thirty-Ninth Street: I was once accused by poet James Den-Boer of mendacity (his word) with regard to this poem. He knows not of what he speaks.

ABOUT THE AUTHOR

James Benton earned his MA in creative writing at Cal State Sacramento, and presently teaches English Writing at Eastern Oregon University. His memoir, poetry, and essays have appeared in numerous literary journals both in print and online. In prior lives, he has worked as a sailor, an electrician, a rock and roll musician, and a private investigator. James currently resides in beautiful La Grande, Oregon.

www.ingramcontent.com/pod-product-compliance
Lightning Source LLC
Chambersburg PA
CBHW051348040426
42453CB00007B/477